Conflict Resolution Solution

Copyright Notice

Copyright © 2015 by Global Courseware, Inc.

All rights reserved. No part of this publication may be reproduced, distributed, or transmitted in any form or by any means, including photocopying, recording, or other electronic or mechanical methods, without the prior written permission of the publisher, except in the case of brief quotations embodied in critical reviews and certain other non-commercial uses permitted by copyright law. Permission requests should be submitted to the publisher in writing at one of the addresses below:

73 Greentree Drive
Suite 68
Dover, Delaware
19904
United States of America

116 Provost Street
New Glasgow, Nova Scotia
B2H 2P4
Canada

CONTENTS

	Preface	7
1	An Introduction to Conflict Resolution	9
2	Conflict Resolution Styles with the Thomas-Kilmann Instrument	17
3	Creating an Effective Atmosphere	25
4	Creating a Mutual Understanding	33
5	Focusing on Individual and Shared Needs	41
6	Getting to the Root Cause	49
7	Generating Options	59
8	Building a Solution	65
9	The Short Version of the Process	71
10	Additional Tools	77

Where all think alike, no one thinks very much.

Walter Lippmann

Preface

Wherever two or more people come together, there is the possibility of conflict. This book will give you a six-step process that you can use to modify and resolve conflicts of any size. You will also learn crucial conflict resolution skills, including dealing with anger and using the Agreement Frame.

Great ideas often receive violent opposition from mediocre minds.

Albert Einstein

Chapter One: An Introduction to Conflict Resolution

People often assume that conflict is always negative. This is not true! People are inherently different, and conflict simply happens when those differences come to light. Viewing conflict in this way can help us maximize the possible positive outcomes of the problem at hand. Equipped with a conflict resolution process, people can explore and understand those differences, and use them to interact in a more positive, productive way.

What is Conflict?

The Random House Dictionary defines conflict as, "to come into collision or disagreement; be contradictory, at variance, or in opposition; clash."

Some examples of conflict can include:

- Two sales representatives are arguing over who gets the latest customer

- A team of employees is upset with their manager over a recent scheduling change

- A group of managers cannot decide who gets the latest project assignment

Conflict can also be healthy. Think about how conflict will increase motivation and competitiveness in these scenarios.

- Two companies vie for the top market share of a particular product
- Several sales teams work to get first place
- Six hockey teams work towards winning a championship

These types of drivers can result in greater success, whether "success" means a better product, better teamwork, better processes, lower prices, trophies, or medals.

Remember, everyone experiences conflict, but how you deal with it, is what matters.

What is Conflict Resolution?

The term "conflict resolution" simply means how you solve conflicts. Although there are many processes available, we have developed one process that you can adapt for any situation. You will even be able to use these tools to prevent conflict and to help others work through conflict.

Some common conflict resolution terms include:

- **Mediation**: It is a process to resolve differences, conducted by an impartial third party.

- **Mediator**: In impartial person who conducts a process to resolve differences.

- **Dispute Resolution**: The name given to any process aimed at resolving differences between two parties.

- **Apparent Conflict**: A situation where the conflict is in the open.

- **Hidden Conflict**: A situation where the conflict is not in the open.

Understanding the Conflict Resolution Process

Conflict can come in many forms, and our process will help you in any situation.

Although we have outlined the various conflict resolution phases in a particular order and with a particular grouping, that doesn't mean that you have to use all the phases all the time.

- **Create an Effective Atmosphere**
    - Neutralize Emotions
    - Set Ground Rules
    - Set the Time and Place

- **Create a Mutual Understanding**
    - Identify Needs for Me, Them, and Us

- **Focus on Individual and Shared Needs**
    - Find Common Ground
    - Build Positive Energy and Goodwill
    - Strengthen the Partnership

- **Get to the Root Cause**
    - Examine Root Causes
    - Create a Fishbone Diagram (for complex issues)
    - Identify Opportunities for Forgiveness
    - Identify the Benefits of Resolution

- **Generate Options**
    - Generate, Don't Evaluate
    - Create Mutual Gain Options and Multiple Option Solutions
    - Dig Deeper into the Options

- **Build a Solution**
    - Create Criteria
    - Create the Shortlist
    - Choose a Solution
    - Build a Plan

Practical Illustration

Todd and Jim had a big problem on their hands. Their supervisor just announced a schedule change that would put them in a time crunch. With so many projects to complete, neither Todd nor Jim thought they'd be able to squeeze everything in and racked their brains trying to figure out how to wrap their heads around their conundrum. Their supervisor, Joe, got wind of their problem and offered to hear them out. Both Todd and Jim harped on the time constraints. Joe shook his head because clearly they were missing the bigger picture. Joe opened their eyes to the possibilities of working more efficiently and being more productive than ever before. Todd and Jim stopped cold. They hadn't considered that option. All in agreement, they abandoned their problem, happy to have a solution at their fingertips.

Pick battles big enough to matter, small enough to win.

Jonathan Kozol

Chapter Two: Conflict Resolution Styles with the Thomas-Kilmann Instrument

There are five widely accepted styles of resolving conflicts. These were originally developed by Kenneth Thomas and Ralph Kilmann in the 1970's. We have even designed our conflict resolution process so that it can be used in conjunction with these styles.

Although we promote the collaborative style throughout this book, there are instances where it is not appropriate (for example, it may be too time-consuming if the issue is relatively insignificant). Understanding all five styles and knowing when to use them is an important part of successful conflict resolution.

Collaborating

With the collaborating approach, the parties work together to develop a win-win solution. This approach promotes assertiveness (rather than aggressiveness or passiveness).

This style is appropriate when:

- The situation is not urgent
- An important decision needs to be made
- The conflict involves a large number of people, or people across different teams
- Previous conflict resolution attempts have failed

This style is not appropriate when:

- A decision needs to be made urgently
- The matter is trivial to all involved

Competing

With a competitive approach, the person in conflict takes a firm stand. They compete with the other party for power, and they typically win (unless they're up against someone else who is competing!) This style is often seen as aggressive, and can often be the cause of other people in the conflict to feeling injured or stepped on.

This style is appropriate when:

- A decision needs to be made quickly (i.e., emergencies)
- An unpopular decision needs to be made
- Someone is trying to take advantage of a situation

This style is not appropriate when:

- People are feeling sensitive about the conflict
- The situation is not urgent

Compromising

With the compromising approach, each person in the conflict gives up something that contributes towards the conflict resolution.

This style is appropriate when:

- A decision needs to be made sooner rather than later (meaning the situation is important but not urgent)
- Resolving the conflict is more important than having each individual "win"
- Power between people in the conflict is equal

This style is not appropriate when:

- A wide variety of important needs must be met
- The situation is extremely urgent
- One person holds more power than another

Accommodating

The accommodating style is one of the most passive conflict resolution styles. With this style, one of the parties in conflict gives up what they want so that the other party can have what they want. In general, this style is not very effective, but it is appropriate in certain scenarios.

This style is appropriate when:

- Maintaining the relationship is more important than winning
- The issue at hand is very important to the other person but is not important to you

This style is not appropriate when:

- The issue is important to you
- Accommodating will not permanently solve the problem

Avoiding

The last approach in the TKI is to avoid the conflict entirely. People who use this style tend to accept decisions without question, avoid confrontation, and delegate difficult decisions and tasks. Avoiding is another passive approach that is typically not effective, but it does have its uses.

This style is appropriate when:

- The issue is trivial
- The conflict will resolve itself on its own soon

This style is not appropriate when:

- The issue is important to you or those close to you (such as your team)
- The conflict will continue or get worse without attention

Practical Illustration

June had fume coming out of her ears. She had exactly one hour to come up with a solution before the walls came tumbling down. With pressure building, June held on firmly to her belief that her idea beat out the competition. Seconds turned to minutes and her coworker, Molly, held her breath, prepared for the solution to roll out of June's mouth. Arms outstretched, her hair in a bunch, June exhaled her solution, nearly bowling Molly over in response. Crisis averted. June once again pushed her ego aside and threw caution to the wind, and threw a mighty solution at the situation. Lucky for all, the solution stuck like glue and everyone breathed a sigh of relief and sang their praises.

Whenever you're in conflict with someone, there is one factor that can make the difference between damaging your relationship and deepening it. That factor is attitude.

William James

Chapter Three: Creating an Effective Atmosphere

When people are involved in a conflict, there is typically a lot of negative energy. Anger, frustration, and disappointment are just a few of the emotions often felt. By establishing a positive atmosphere, we can begin to turn that negative energy around, and create a powerful problem-solving force. This creates a strong beginning for the conflict resolution process.

Neutralizing Emotions

Before beginning the conflict resolution process, both parties must agree that they want to resolve the conflict. Without this crucial buy-in step, achieving a win-win solution is close to impossible.

Once participants have agreed to resolve the conflict, it is important to neutralize as many negative emotions as possible. This means giving the participants in the conflict time to vent and work through the feelings associated with the conflict.

Key steps for the people in conflict include:

- Accept that you have negative feelings and that these feelings are normal.

- Acknowledge the feelings and their root causes. Example: "I feel very angry about the way George spoke to me in that meeting."

- Identify how you might resolve your feelings. Example: "If George apologized to me, I would feel a lot better."

- This can generate ideas about what the root cause of the conflict is, and how to resolve it. Example: "George and I haven't been getting along very well since the merger. I wonder if he might be having some stress and anxiety."

Setting Ground Rules

Ground rules provide a framework for people to resolve their conflict. Ground rules should be set at the beginning of any conflict resolution process. They can be very brief or very detailed – whatever the situation requires.

Ground rules should be:

- Developed and agreed upon by both parties.
- Positive when it is possible. (For example, "We will listen to each other's statements fully," rather than, "We will not interrupt.")
- Fair to both parties
- Enforceable
- Adjustable
- Written and posted somewhere where both parties can refer to it (for more formal dispute resolution processes).

If the parties are using a mediator to help them resolve the conflict, it is important that the ground rules be developed by the parties and not the mediator. The mediator's role is that of a guide and mentor, not a judge or supreme ruler.

Some examples of ground rules include:

- We will listen to each other's statements fully before responding.
- We will work together to achieve a mutually acceptable solution.
- We will respect each other as individuals, and therefore not engage in personal insults and attacks.

Participants can use the ground rules throughout the conflict resolution process to monitor and modify their behaviors. Ground rules give participants an objective, logical way of addressing personal attacks and emotional issues.

An example: "Joe, I feel like you have cut off my last several statements. We agreed at the beginning of this that we would listen to each other's statements fully before answering."

If the conflict is being mediated, this also gives the mediator a fair way to give participants feedback and help them work with the conflict. Since the same rules are being applied to everyone, it can help the mediator maintain fairness and avoid bias.

Choosing the Time and Place

The right time and place is often a key part of resolving conflict. Trying to solve a major team issue five minutes before the end of the shift just isn't going to work – people are going to be focused on going home, not on the problem.

When possible, choose a quiet place to discuss the conflict. Make sure that there is lots of time allowed. Minimize distractions if possible: turn cell phones off, forward office phones to voice mail, and turn off computers.

If you are mediating a conflict resolution meeting, be conscious of the needs of both parties when scheduling the meeting. Make sure that the time chosen works well for both of them. Choose a location that is neutral (one that they are both comfortable with or that neither has visited before). Removing distractions will enable both parties to concentrate on the matter at hand: resolving the conflict.

Practical Illustration

Cal fumed with anger. He could see no light at the end of the tunnel. James felt that he lost his footing on the project as well. Cal and James hemmed and hawed like children in a school yard because each wanted to be right. Their boss, Mildred, heard the word war and marched right in to nip it in the bud. Mildred knew that the only solution would be for both Cal and James to meet in the middle. They lined up their points and studied each fragment until they found a middle ground they could both walk on without feeling like they were going to topple over. Mildred applauded their efforts and rewarded them with a pat on the back to show her appreciation for a job well done.

Conflict is inevitable, but combat is optional.

Max Lucade

Chapter Four: Creating a Mutual Understanding

There is an old story about two girls arguing over an orange. They both wanted this single orange to themselves. They argued for hours over who should get it and why. Finally, though, they realized that they could both win: one wanted the rind for a cake, while the other one wanted to make juice from the inside of the orange.

This model of win-win situations and mutual gain is our preferred outcome for any conflict. In this Chapter, we will explore how creating mutual understanding can lay the groundwork for a win-win solution.

What Do I Want?

To begin, identify what you personally want out of the conflict. Try to state this positively.

Examples:

- I want a fair share of all new customers.
- I want a better working relationship with my manager.
- I want changes to the schedule.

You can create two versions of your personal needs statement: your ideal resolution and your realistic resolution. Alternatively, you could frame your statement into several steps if the conflict is complicated.

Another useful exercise is to break down your statement into wants and needs. This is particularly valuable if your statement is vague. Let's take the statement, "I want changes to the schedule," as an example.

Want	Need
More input into the scheduling process	To work less than 30 hours per week
A more regular schedule	More notice for schedule changes

This will give you some bargaining room during the conflict resolution process, and will help ensure that you get what you need out of the solution. In the example above, you may be willing to give up a more regular schedule if more notice for schedule changes is provided.

What Do They Want?

Next, identify what the person that you are in conflict with wants. Try to frame this positively. Explore all the angles to maximize your possibilities for mutual gain.

These framing questions will help you start the process.

- What does my opponent need?
- What does my opponent want?
- What is most important to them?
- What is least important to them?

What Do We Want?

Now that you have identified the wants and needs of both sides, look for areas of overlap. These will be the starting points for establishing mutual ground.

Here is an example. Joe and George are in conflict over the current schedule. As the most senior members of the assembly line team, they both alternate their regular duties with that of supervisor. Although taking on the responsibility gives the supervisor an extra $250 per shift, the supervisor also has to work an extra hour per shift, and has additional safety responsibilities.

Joe and George both work Monday to Friday, and as a regular assembly line team member, their shifts are from 8:30 a.m. to 4:30 p.m. As supervisor, they are expected to work from 8 a.m. to 5 p.m.

	Joe	George
Wants	To have at least two supervisor shifts per week.	To have at least two supervisor shifts per week. To leave by 4:30 p.m. on Fridays.
Needs	To leave by 4:30 p.m. on Mondays and Wednesdays to pick up his children. To ensure that the foreman position is covered by someone from Monday to Friday, 8 a.m. to 5 p.m.	Not to have more than three supervisor shifts per week as it will require him to pay extra taxes. To ensure that the foreman position is covered by someone from Monday to Friday, 8 a.m. to 5 p.m.

From this simple chart, we can see that Joe and George have the same goal: to ensure that the supervisor position is covered by someone during regular working hours. Thus, this is a logistical conflict rather than an emotional one. We can also see from the chart that there seems to be some good starting ground for a solution.

When working through the wants and needs of both parties, be careful not to jump to conclusions. Rather, be on the lookout for the root cause. Often, the problem is not what it seems.

Practical Illustration

Tim kicked the vending machine. Nate covered his ears at the noise thundering around the office. Tim stomped across the floor and slammed his office door behind him. Wondering what had gotten Tim's goat, Nate tip-toed over and offered a wide grin. Tim's scowl told Nate that Tim had reached his boiling point and needed help fast. Nate tried to pry information from the steaming Tim asking, "What got under your craw? It can't be the vending machine or the door. Spill the beans." Tim's hunched shoulders fell as he let the truth spill out of his grimacing mouth. "I need help with this project." Relieved that his head didn't get ripped off, Nate said, "Well, it's your lucky day! I'm just the man to solve this problem. Step aside and allow me to take the monkey off your back."

Good battle is objective and honest, never vicious or cruel.

Ann Landers

Chapter Five: Focusing on Individual and Shared Needs

So far, we have talked about laying the foundation for common ground, one of the key building blocks for win-win solutions. This Chapter will look at some techniques on building common ground and using it to create partnerships.

It may not seem like we have progressed very far in resolving the conflict. Indeed, most of these primary steps are focused on information gathering and problem solving. For minor conflicts, having these steps in your toolbox will simply help you keep all possibilities in mind during the conflict. For major conflicts, these steps will help you ensure you achieve the best solution possible for the situation.

Finding Common Ground

We have already talked about finding common ground when exploring each side's wants and needs. With these tools, you should be able to find common ground even before the conflict begins.

In our earlier example, with Joe and George in conflict over the supervisor schedule, they both wanted to ensure that the position was covered during their hours of responsibility. Other possible areas of common ground could include ensuring the safety of the assembly line team, continuing to work with each other, or continuing to work for the company. Try hard enough and you'll find something in common!

You should continue to try to find common ground throughout the entire conflict resolution process. It will help you understand your adversary's position and better position you to help create a win-win solution. These positive gestures will build goodwill, and help you make the shift from being two people in conflict to being two people working to solve a problem.

Some examples:

- "I think the company needs a more unified sales team, too."

- "I would really like us to win first place this year, too."

- "I agree that we can get this conflict resolved and build a better widget."

Building Positive Energy and Goodwill

There are often many negative emotions associated with conflict. No wonder – conflict makes many people upset and anxious, and often results in negative feelings like anger and disappointment.

If you are able to turn that negative energy into positive energy to help build goodwill with the person that you are in conflict with, resolving the conflict will be much easier. Ironically, the more negative the situation, the more important this step is.

Let's say that the person that you are in conflict with is very angry with you. Although they have agreed that they want to resolve the conflict, they are cool towards you and putting in minimum effort towards resolving the problem.

You may think, "Why should I bother?" This is a very important question indeed. How much energy and time are you will to spend on this conflict? Is it worth resolving? (We will explore these questions more in the next Chapter.)

Consider, however, the power that your approach has. You have two basic options: to match your adversary's demeanor, or to be a positive influence. Both will likely take as much energy, but which will yield greater results?

Here are some ways to build positive energy.

- Have a good attitude. The preparation steps we discussed earlier should help you identify the positive things that will come out of this conflict. Try to focus on these things instead of the negative aspects of the conflict.
- Frame things positively.
- Create actionable items.
- Try to keep emotions out of your statements. State feelings and opinions in as objective a manner as possible. Label your thoughts as thoughts by starting sentences with, "I think…"
- Take a break when you need it.
- If you say, "I see where you're coming from," make sure you mean it. If you can't see where they are coming from, ask them to tell you more. Often, sharing information can break down even the toughest person's defenses.
- Invite the other person to step into your shoes. Tell them a story, outline consequences, and explain how you feel in an objective manner. Share as much information as you can.

Strengthening Your Partnership

Making the transition from opponents to problem-solving teammates is one of the most powerful conflict resolution tools. We have already discussed ways to build common ground to help bridge the gap between you and the person having the conflict. These tools are a great start, but there are some additional things that you can do to maintain and strengthen that partnership.

In 1965, Bruce Tuckman, developed a four-stage model showing how teams grow and develop. This model can be applied to one-on-one human interactions, too.

Stage	Explanation	What You Can Do to Help
Forming	Team members are just meeting, unsure of their role and themselves.	Encourage team building through non-conflict laden tasks and activities. Involve the team in task planning and goal setting.
Storming	Team members discover differences and butt heads; conflict can interfere with progress.	Continue with the plan; evaluate and adjust as necessary. Support the team through conflict and help them resolve it.

Norming	Team members start to discover similarities too. Performance typically improves, but social interaction may also cause it to drop.	Keep the group focused on the goal; encourage social activities outside of team time.
Performing	Team members are now comfortable with each other and work together well.	Continue to offer resources and support to the team. Monitor performance, as teams can change stages at any time (particularly when members join in or drop out).

Practical Illustration

Malcolm whisked passed his coworker, Randy. Malcolm's blood still boiled over being forced to work as a team with the Randy. Malcolm saw himself as an island. He stood his ground and refused to help Randy with any of the project at hand. Randy watched in wonder as Malcolm paraded his passive-aggressive behavior around the office. Randy decided the time had come to put a stop to the madness and forged a solution that would leave both productive and happy. With a few kind words spewed at Malcolm, the thick air between them wafted out the door, leaving them to put their heads together and work in harmony or risk losing more than their tempers. In record time, working together, Malcolm and Randy produced immaculate work, worthy of a standing ovation.

*Peace is not the absence of conflict,
but the ability to cope with it.*

Anonymous

Chapter Six: Getting to the Root Cause

Building a positive foundation and gathering information are key steps to resolving conflict, but it is going to be difficult to solve the problem if we don't know what the problem is! In this Chapter, we will learn how to delve below the current conflict to the root of the problem. This phase is important for long-term resolution, rather than a band-aid solution.

Examining Root Causes

Once the groundwork has been laid, it is important to look at the root causes of the conflict.

One way to do this is through simple verbal investigation. This involves continuously asking "Why?" to get to the root of the problem. An example:

- I was very upset when Sharon vetoed my idea at the meeting.
- Why <were you upset>?
- I felt that my idea had real value and she didn't listen to what I had to say.
- Why <didn't she listen to what you had to say>?
- She has been with the company for a lot longer than I have and I feel that she doesn't respect me.

Now we have progressed from a single isolated incident to the root cause of the incident itself (and probably many more past and future incidents). Resolving this root cause will provide greater value and satisfaction to all involved.

Paying attention to the wording of the root cause is important, too.

- Watch out for vague verbs.
- Try to keep emotions out of the problem statements.

Creating a Cause and Effect Diagram

Another way of examining root causes is to create a cause and effect diagram (also known as a fishbone diagram) with the person that you are having the conflict. To start, draw a horizontal arrow pointing to the right on a large sheet of paper. At the end of the arrow, write down the problem.

Now, work together to list possible causes. Group these causes. Draw a line pointing to the large arrow for each cause and write the cause at the top.

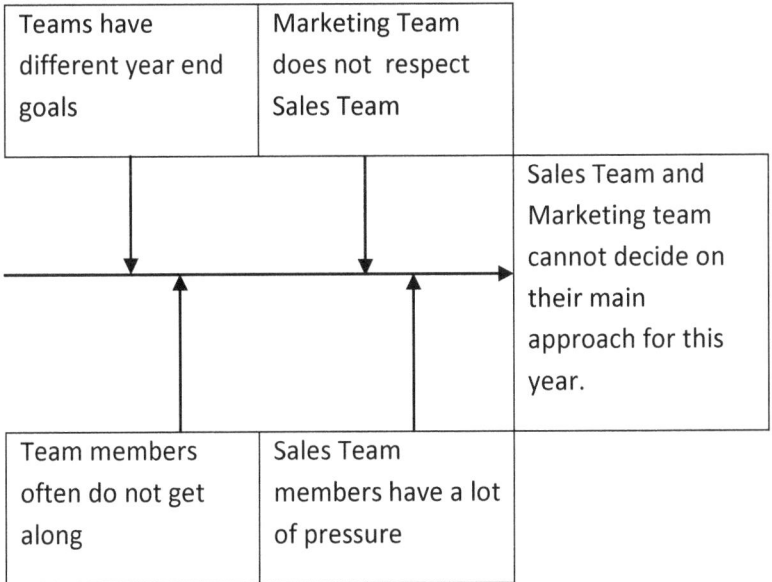

Now, write each cause on a line pointing to the group arrow. (Sticky notes work well for this.)

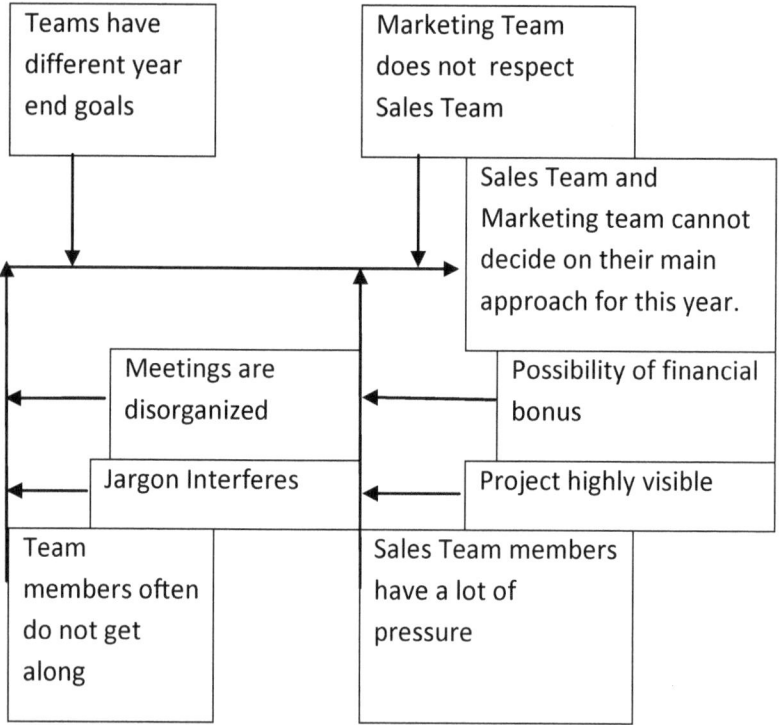

Now the people in the conflict have a clear map of what is happening.

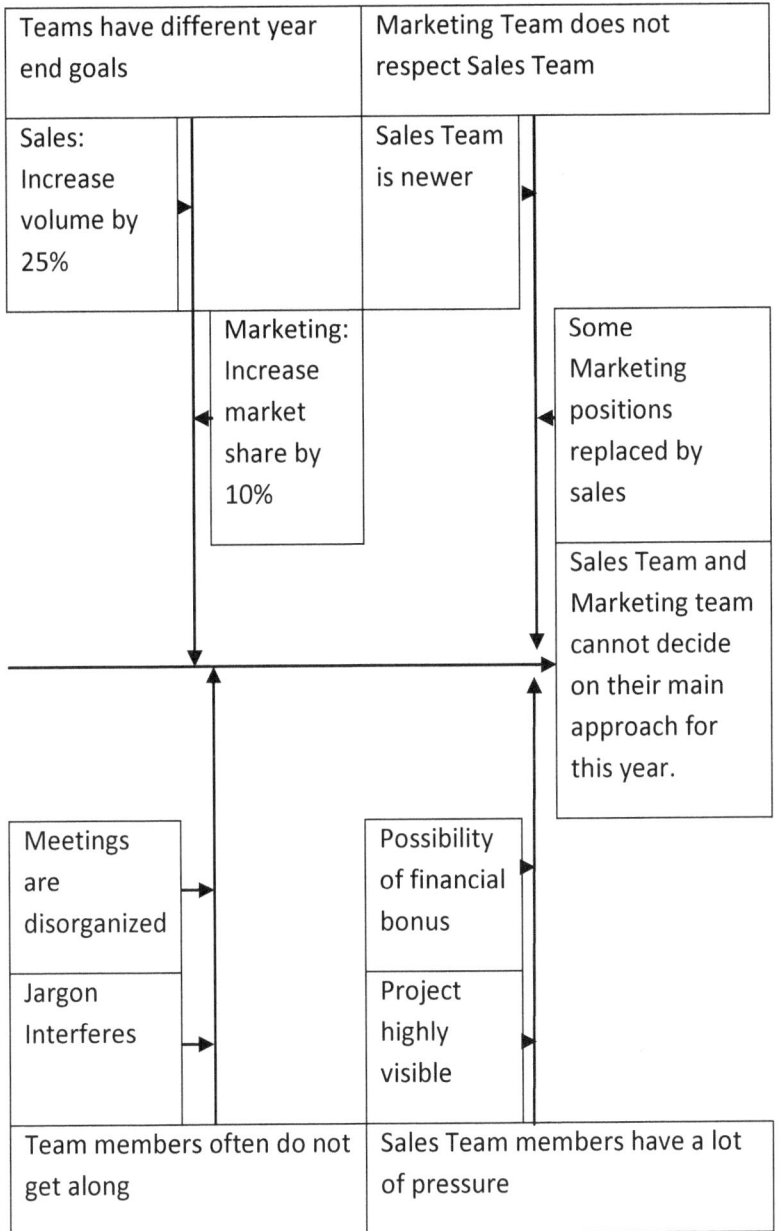

Although this technique can be time-consuming, it is excellent for complicated conflicts or for team conflicts where there may be more than one root cause. The drawing should be updated as new causes are discovered.

The Importance of Forgiveness

Forgiveness is a key concept in conflict resolution. Forgiveness does not mean forgetting that the conflict happened, or erasing the emotions that it created. It does mean accepting that the conflict happened. Accepting and working through how it made you feel, accepting the consequences that it had, and letting those actions and consequences exist in the past.

Successful conflict resolution should give the participants some feeling of closure over the issue. Participants should feel that the conflict has been resolved to their satisfaction, and that it will not likely reoccur. These accomplishments should help participants put the conflict behind them and move forward, to more things that are positive.

These goals should be kept in mind during the resolution process. Ask yourself, "Will resolving this help provide me with closure? Will this action help me accept what has happened and move on?"

Identifying the Benefits of Resolution

There is no doubt about it – conflict resolution can be hard work. Effective conflict resolution digs deep into the issues, often exploring unfamiliar territory, to resolve the core conflict and prevent the problem from reoccurring.

However, this process can be time-consuming and emotionally difficult. You and the person that you are in conflict with may arrive at a point (or several points) in the conflict resolution process where you wonder, "Is this really worth it?"

When you arrive at these stalemates, look at why you are resolving the conflict. It can also be helpful to explore what will happen if the conflict is not resolved.

- What relationships will deteriorate or break up?
- If this is a workplace conflict, what is the financial cost to the company?
- What will be the emotional cost to the participants?
- Who else will be affected?

These questions should help participants put things into perspective and evaluate whether or not the conflict is truly worth resolving. In most situations, resolving the true conflict is well worth the effort in the long term. Visualizing the benefits can provide the motivation to work through the rest of the process.

For complex conflicts, there are some additional ways to stay motivated. It's OK to break the resolution sessions into parts, with a different goal for each session. It's also OK to take breaks as needed – a walk around the block or a glass of water can do wonders to refresh the mind and body.

Practical Illustration

Marty cringed at the sound of Justin's paddle slamming on the table. Marty's proposal denied again. Marty sat with his mouth open, unable to imagine what could have gone wrong this time. Justin saw a hint of frustration in Marty's eyes and snickered to himself. Marty noticed the sly grin splashed across Justin's face and gathered his strength to ask the question. "Why?" He asked. Surprised by Marty's question, Justin shot up in his seat and declared a hearty, "Because I said so!" Not satisfied with that response, Marty investigated further. Both Marty and Justin verbally squabbled until Marty had enough and declared a truce. The clock chimed behind them. Marty grabbed his paddle and shot it into the air. "Why?" It read. Justin shrugged because he didn't have an answer. Both men laughed and shook on it. The debate no longer a problem and the proposal accepted.

It's not what you look at that matters, it's what you see.

Henry David Thoreau

Chapter Seven: Generating Options

Once you have a good handle on the conflict, it's time for all parties in conflict to start generating some options for resolution. In this stage, it's all about quantity, not quality; you want as many options to choose from as possible.

Generate, Don't Evaluate

To begin, generate ideas for resolving the symptoms of the conflict. Then, move on to the root cause and expand your list of ideas.

Don't be afraid to throw out wacky ideas or to ask, "What if?" Remember, this stage is about what you can do, not what you will do.

It is very important not to censor yourself or the person that you are having the conflict. Record all possible ideas into a list or brainstorming diagram. If you have created a cause and effect diagram, you can record ideas for resolution right on the diagram. (Once again, sticky notes are ideal for this initial, idea-generating phase.)

At this stage, all your work to build common ground and positive relationships will really start to pay off. As you and the person you are in conflict with start to generate options, the positive energy will build, increasing your creative output exponentially.

If you are having trouble thinking of solutions, use these questions to jump-start your creativity.

- In an ideal world, how would this conflict be resolved?
- How do we not want this conflict to be resolved?
- How might others resolve this conflict?

Creating Mutual Gain Options and Multiple Option Solutions

Once you have a good list of options, look over the list, and perform some basic evaluation.

- Cross off options that are an absolute no-go for either party.
- Highlight options that provide gains for both parties.
- Look for options that can be combined for an optimal solution.
- Make options more detailed where appropriate.
- Continue brainstorming and generating ideas.

What if your entire list of options gets crossed off? Then it's back to the drawing board! If you are having trouble coming up with ideas, consider taking a quick break, moving the brainstorming meeting elsewhere, and/or involving outside parties.

Digging Deeper into Your Options

Once the list has been narrowed down, dig deeper into each option and identify the following:

- The effort for each option (perhaps on a scale of one to ten)
- The payback for each option (also on a scale of one to ten)
- Your estimation as to its likelihood of success
- Other options that could be used to complement it
- Each party's preference for it (expressed as yes/no, or a percentage in favor)

At this point, we are still gathering information and exploring options, so try to make the list as long as possible. For simple conflicts, three to five options is usually sufficient, but with more complex issues, five to eight options may be necessary. If the team involves more than two people, you will likely need eight to twelve options.

Practical Illustration

Vern kept his mouth zipped shut during the meeting. He didn't want to rock the boat with his fantastic new ideas. Seth, Vern's boss, waxed poetic about his own ideas. Vern sank lower and lower into the abyss of ideas not shared. His coworker Joanne threw Vern a lifeline and stated that the meeting should come to a halt. All eyes were on the crimson faced Vern. He cleared his throat, sat up taller in his seat, and began to give the speech of his lifetime. A fuming Seth tried to inject with 'But, wait" and "What about me?", but no one noticed. All in the room hung on Vern's every word. His confidence renewed, Vern gave wonderfully detailed data about his idea and won the praises of those around him. Nearly a foot taller as he soaked in the adulation, Vern could stand proud of himself for conquering his fear and making a name for himself.

The harder the conflict, the more glorious the triumph.

Thomas Paine

Chapter Eight: Building a Solution

Once the possible solutions are laid out, it's time to move on to choosing a solution and laying the groundwork for a resolution. This Chapter will explore how to create criteria and how to use those criteria to create a shortlist of options, and then to move on to a solution.

Creating Criteria

For the moment, set aside your list of options. It's time to create a framework to evaluate those options. Try not to think about the different options as you create the criteria. Focus instead on the wants and needs of both parties.

Criteria should explore what you want and do not want from the solution. You can also prioritize your criteria by what is necessary to have and what you would like to have (also known as needs and wants). Identify any items on the list you would be willing to make a compromise with.

Criteria	Want?	Need?	Shared with Opponent?	Compromise On?

The best approach is for each party to take a few moments to write down their individual criteria, and then come together and combine the lists to create a final set of criteria. Although it is important to work together on this list, it is also important that the wants and needs of both parties be respected.

You may ask, why create criteria after creating options? Wouldn't it make more sense to create a list of criteria and then generate a list of options?

Logically, this approach does make more sense. However, it can be difficult to come up with creative options when you already have a framework in mind. Therefore, we recommend brainstorming first, and then creating criteria second.

Creating a Shortlist

Once the criteria have been created, bring out the list of solutions. Eliminate any solutions that do not match the must-have criteria that you and your partner identified. At the end of this process, you should have a small, manageable list of potential solutions.

You may find that there are no solutions left after this process. There are two options in this case. One is to re-evaluate your criteria and re-evaluate the solutions, to ensure there really are no options left. Another is to go back to the drawing board and work on additional solution ideas.

Choosing a Solution

Now, choose a final solution. Remember, you can often combine multiple options for even greater success!

Here is a checklist to evaluate the chosen solution.

- Is it a win-win solution for everyone involved?
- Are all needs provided for?
- Are all criteria met?

Building a Plan

Now, let's create a plan to put the solution in action. The complexity of this plan should vary with the complexity of the situation. For simple conflicts, you may frame an agreement like this: "Janice and I will take turns taking new customers, and we will make sure that we let each other know when this happens."

With complex situations, such as those involving a group of people or multiple option solutions, a detailed action plan may be appropriate. It is important that each party take responsibility for implementing the solution, even if it is determined that one party is at fault.

For example, let's say that the conflict resolution process has determined that communication issues between Janet and Susan are causing most of the conflict over new customer assignment. Although Janet and Susan are going to work on this problem by improving communication and keeping fairness in mind, the remainder of the team will be responsible for supporting Janet and Susan and following up to make sure no further issues arise.

The action plan should also include a list of things to do if the conflict is not actually resolved after implementing the solution. Typically, the parties will re-evaluate the cause and effect diagram to ensure their analysis of the root cause was accurate. They may also want to examine their criteria and explore other solutions.

Practical Illustration

Thomas had a huge mountain of work to climb. He scratched his head and hoped that a solution would fall from the sky and land right in the palm of his hands. His coworker, Mason explained that that's not how the world works. Mason gave Thomas a reality check by explaining that in order for something to be done, Thomas had to get up and make it happen. Thomas frowned and furrowed his brows. In his mind, a solution seemed more impossible a feat than the mountain of work he had to climb to even begin to think about how to solve bigger problems. Mason recognized the worry written all over Thomas' face and made a road map for Thomas to follow if he had any intention of getting any work done. Thomas reluctantly followed the map and in the blink of an eye found that he could not only get through the hill in front of him, but that he could conquer any obstacle that got in his way.

Seek first to understand, then to be understood.

Stephen Covey

Chapter Nine: The Short Version of the Process

So far, we have explored the six phases of the conflict resolution process in depth. As we discussed earlier, these phases can be adapted for virtually any type of conflict. In this Chapter, we will work through an abridged version of the processes that can be used easily to successfully resolve conflicts. We will also look at some individual steps that can be used as conflict resolution and prevention tools.

Evaluating the Situation

To begin, we will combine all the groundwork into a single step.

- **Phase One** (Creating an Effective Atmosphere): Take a moment to calm down and deal with your emotions. Look at the possible positive outcomes of the conflict.

- **Phase Two** (Creating a Mutual Understanding): Quickly evaluate your wants and needs, and those of the other party. Try to identify the real issue.

- **Phase Three** (Focusing on Individual and Shared Goals): Identify common ground.

This information can be gathered in just a few moments, and it will help you identify the most appropriate conflict resolution approach. (Remember the five approaches that we looked at in Chapter Two.) Although we promote the collaborative approach, there are situations where other approaches are more appropriate and beneficial.

Choosing Your Steps

Now, let's work through phases four and five. Think about the current conflict. Is it really the root cause or is it just a symptom of a larger problem? (Most often, it's just a symptom.) How could the problem be resolved?

Make a short list of possible solutions, even if it's just in your head. Now we're ready to move on to the next phases.

Creating an Action Plan

Once you have some ideas on how to resolve the conflict, do a quick evaluation. What do you want and need out of the solution? What might the other party need? Use these to sketch out a solution. (Remember, if you're going to propose a solution, the other party is going to want to know what's in it for them, so make sure you have something to offer.)

Have a backup plan, too, in case your approach doesn't work. This could be a different solution, a different way of presenting your original solution, or even a proposal to move to a more complex resolution process. Simply have some ideas in your back pocket in case your original approach doesn't work.

Using Individual Process Steps

In this book, we have outlined the various conflict resolution phases in a particular order and with a particular grouping. That doesn't mean that you have to use all the phases all the time. Most of the items we have discussed can be used individually as conflict prevention or resolution tools.

Here are some examples.

- A new person has joined your team. She is very quiet and the team (yourself included) is having a hard time getting to know and like her. You use some of the tools we discussed today to build common ground with her and improve teamwork.

- Lately, team status meetings have gotten out of hand. People talk over each other, argue constantly, and often leave the room. You suggest implementing ground rules for these meetings.

- One of your colleagues often behaves very aggressively. You find it very difficult to communicate with him because you find him so intimidating. You use emotional neutralization techniques to focus on your message and reduce the impact of his behavior.

Practical Illustration

Ruben stormed out of the meeting in a heated rush. Paul tried to stop him, but his words of wisdom flew right over Ruben's head. Ruben didn't want his schedule to be changed, but he had no words to explain his dilemma. Instead, he huffed and puffed until he couldn't take it anymore and the pressure cooker in his mind exploded in other ways. Ruben would scream, shout, pout, and ignore Paul's attempts to help. Paul finally cornered Ruben and made him listen to reason. A few minutes of smoke billowing out of his ears and Ruben started to see the error in his ways. Ruben's furrowed brows relaxed and his tense shoulders gave way to a new emotion. Paul's words were turning Ruben's frown upside down once Ruben admitted what really had him upset and let go of the angry cobwebs that were clouding his perception.

You can't shake hands with a clenched fist.

Indira Gandhi

Chapter Ten: Additional Tools

To help wrap up this book, we would like to share some additional tools that can help you resolve conflicts.

Stress and Anger Management Techniques

There is no doubt about it – dealing with conflict can be hard on the mind and the body. Being well equipped with some stress and anger management techniques can help you stay calm during the conflict resolution process. Nothing is going to get solved when either (or both) parties are angry and upset.

Here are some tips to help keep you cool during the conflict resolution process.

- Deep breathing has beneficial mental and physical effects.

- Coping thoughts can help you stay calm, too. Some examples: "I feel like he is just trying to push my buttons. I'm stronger than that!" or, "I'm not going to let myself get upset – that won't solve anything. Instead, I am going to focus on getting this conflict solved."

- Make sure to take breaks as needed. If the person you are in conflict with becomes emotional or stressed, encourage them to take breaks as well.

- After the conflict is over, talk about it with someone appropriate.

The Agreement Frame

The Agreement Frame can be used in any situation to explain your viewpoint in an assertive, non-confrontational way, without watering your position down. It is designed to encourage discussion and information sharing between all parties. Although it can be used in many situations, it is particularly effective in conflict resolution.

The Agreement Frame takes one of three forms:

- I appreciate, and...
- I respect, and...
- I agree, and...

Here is an example of the Agreement Frame in use.

Person A	Person B
The best way to resolve this conflict is for you to resign your position immediately.	I respect your opinion, and I think that there might be some other viable options.
What options were you considering?	I think that if I issued an apology to the team for the misunderstanding that we would be on our way to resolving the conflict.
I think that option is too low-key for this situation.	I agree that it might not be a strong enough statement, and I may need to have team meetings to address the underlying issues.

Remember, the words "but" and "however" are conversation-stoppers. Try to avoid using them with the agreement frame.

Asking Open Questions

When possible, use the five W's or the H to ask a question.

- Who?
- What?
- Where?
- When?
- Why?
- How?

These questions encourage discussion, self-evaluation, and open conversation. Some useful questions for conflict resolution include:

- What happened?
- Why do you feel that way?
- When did this problem start?
- How does that make you feel?
- Who else is involved?

Practical Illustration

Raymond couldn't seem to catch his breath. He spent his day dripping beads of sweat. Nancy knew Raymond had a problem with stress. Raymond carried stress like a monkey on his back. Nancy understood that if she allowed her coworker to continue ignoring the real problem, Raymond would back himself into a corner. Nancy decided the time had come to step in and play the hero instead of letting Raymond roll the dice with his life. Nancy took her chipper attitude and raced into Raymond's cubicle. Nancy told Raymond that he needed a break and that a brisk walk around the office would clear his head and help him out of his funk. Raymond scowled but agreed. Three quick sprints around the office left Raymond winded, but his head felt clearer and he had more energy. Nancy gave him the push he needed to get more done minus the headaches.

The quality of our lives depends not on whether or not we have conflicts, but on how we respond to them.

Tom Crum

Closing Thoughts

- **William Ellery Channing**: Difficulties are meant to rouse, not discourage. The human spirit is to grow strong by conflict.

- **M. Esther Harding**: Conflict is the beginning of consciousness.

- **Carl W. Buechner**: They may forget what you said, but they will never forget how you made them feel.

www.ingramcontent.com/pod-product-compliance
Lightning Source LLC
Chambersburg PA
CBHW041102180526
45172CB00001B/65